LIMBS OF THE APPLE TREE NEVER DIE

LIMBS OF THE APPLE TREE NEVER DIE

JOEL FELIX

VERGE BOOKS / CHICAGO

This book, wherever it goes,
is for CANDICE RAI,
who was waiting there.

LIMBS OF THE APPLE TREE NEVER DIE

FIELD BOOK: CAIRO

Two kids fish under a bridge from the hood of a car. A flick of the line and a new worm test a spot where the Mississippi and Ohio rivers combine. I stop to see what they got and watch the tuck and pull of the river tense the poles. No vision can trace the folds of force where rivers meet. And all the rivers of the world meet underground, I remember from Virgil. We see this in the eyes of Aristaeus, the distraught farmer who cries out to his mother, immortal Cyrene below the waters, when the bees in his orchard have failed. Cyrene pulls Aristaeus down to her throne by parting the river and *arching the wave mountain-like round about him.* His body was brought down, as in a vase. He fell among the sorting waves within the water, tassels of foam tracing the fall of mountains underground, at last to Cyrene's granite vault where he *gazed on all the rivers, as, each in its own place, glides under the great earth.* How is this not the descent of the lyric mind, plumbing the conditions that birthed it?—I write, the breeze flipping the edge of the page.

I am outside the small town of Cairo, on the southern tip of Illinois as drawn by the rivers. I'm heading south to Alabama on a Self-Guided Civil Rights Tour, but stopped here with the sudden recollection that Cairo was where Jim and Huck Finn thought they could raft upstream, slipping off the Mississippi and up the Ohio, to freedom. Hard to imagine the image of liberation, driving around on this day. Once a bustling border town, Cairo suffers from waves of disinvestment from the retreat of river and rail commerce and a bitter history of racial violence. A shrunken population, over 60 percent African American, means a shrinking tax base, and Cairo struggles to meet basic civic demands of public utilities and repair while under constant threat, as always, of more flood.

In the center of town you look north to the see the South, as the rivers wedged this part of Illinois below a jut of Kentucky. Power creates many forms of enslavement, but this brown river once held all the desperate hope of deliverance from the horror of slavery. What is lost when we lose the horror that once made this boundary terrible? And what is the point of an art that can't touch the living wound of this history?

The condition of the lyric mind moves through a time of rhetorical war over the instrumental power of critical consciousness to describe what freedom meant and means. I'm driven south by an inchoate need to connect to fields of courage of the civil rights battle, partly because I am numbed to that history all around me where I lived. I was not far from the crisply maintained headquarters of the Nation of Islam in Chicago, where Elijah Muhammad settled when forced from Detroit. For all its power as a sign, the near and more distant histories of the Nation of Islam were intangible in Chicago's daily hustle for cash. The grant and refusal of freedom is most firmly felt in the competitions of economic class, even if it is an ambivalent, disordered construct at the very base of rationality. The escape from slavery, the justice claim of legal remediation from the social instruments of racial oppression, protection of independent cultural economies of belief, leisure to let the mind wander on a day off: all proposals of freedom remain grants of power, and daily life takes place within the push and pull between power and the quasi-articulable belief that freedom is an ordained, inextricable right of any one human body.

Our disordered rationality unfolds as empire. Whenever convenient, the freedom concept is relicensed as a military directive fused to continuous market expansion. Recent rhetorics of power no longer flinch at claiming war as an extension of the civil rights era, and no one protests. Michael Gerson, George W. Bush's principal speechwriter, saw American civil rights marches in the bombing and invasion of Iraq. When re-elected by the war created, Bush used the occasion of his second inaugural speech in 2005 to fantasize a connection between the "Freedom Now" desegregation protests of the 1960s and his presumed liberated Iraqi citizens post-Hussein.

I head back to the Interstate. In the 2011 floods, Cairo was mostly evacuated as the levees were overtopped and the Mississippi recorded its highest mark on record. With the very existence of the town at stake, the Army Corps of Engineers blew levees along the Mississippi flood plain, saving Cairo, and temporarily ruining some Missouri corn and soybean farmland downstream. It was one or the other. Days before, the Missouri Speaker of the House was asked his view of which should be sacrificed, the town or the farmland: "Cairo. I've been there, trust me. Cairo. Have you been to Cairo?" he added. "OK, then you know what I'm saying then."

WINESAP (APPLE)

a living limb from the Winesap tree
  long dead
       will produce Winesap from memory
         in any unknown root

              nobody knows how

AFTER LIBERTY HYDE BAILEY (1928)

GRIMES GOLDEN
(APPLE)

Precocious oblate acid notes,

what *terroir* took up
in Wellsburg, West Virginia

's ancient, single-tree ciders?

Drip,
vinous sport, for which pope
brings welcome giving?

To where do we follow
thy profusion

of crime-goldened days,
snuffle wind-fall
trails

of pin lights
pillow-stitched in the
tilth?

LEAST WIND

in least wind
yarrow stalks
dippin sticks
for ages a rain
O drum frog

era is ova
drew the tea clear
air then air
two scale trees and wet hair
lick your face

ON PHARMAKOS FARM

FOR TOM

Join my song

flossing loopholes

'neath this spiny tree

for time has difficulty

rolling uphill—

nothing consecutive

on this cloud-imitated mountain:

cluster and

clearing

blue flashes

on the backs of birds

the sound of cinnamon

all you get

till you're picked

on *pharmakos* farm

no cooling herb

from bloodless flowers

at the bottom of summer's

paper hearts

THE HOUSE IS
HOSTILITY

To be taught the cello
is to fall in love
with the force of causing love
on your street
yet neither is remedy
for the house,
nor what it
　　　stood for.

MATHEW BRADY
POSES THE DEAD

this one almost a womanly lament
two hands clapped to the gun barrel
like the last bar of his jail
something puckish in his mate
cap askew, cap backwards, capping musket end
foe's cap peaking from the mud
the viscera tipped out
locked arm in arm
almost sleeping on the pillow of the eyes
boot in the high grass
a hand without author
sinking muscle and meat
to bones coming out like rock on a ridge
followed a sow to the great stench
a poor parody
too little drama fails the truth

rain spoiled the work of hours

no light to capture

little cooling breeze

as my assistant abandoned me

on a crumbling verge

whistled to calm my nerves

the hole in that soldier's head might whistle

like the whistle hole in my face

hear me whistle little head hole, my God, *blow*

in my hole

FIELD BOOK:
PHARSALIA

Leaving the long flood plains of the Mississippi with my two companions: Martin Luther King Jr.'s *Why We Can't Wait* and Lucan's epic Latin poem *De Bello Civili*. Seemingly worlds away, these texts test the coherence of the dialectic so tempting to the franchise of freedom. "Franchise," should it connote pop-up architecture and fast food in the vernacular, was early associated with "freedom" in that the term came from the Roman name for the people that remained free from control and taxation, the *Franc*, who were in turn named after their tool of freedom, throwing axes called the *francisca*, bane of the Centurion. On this green and violet dusk in the middle of the country, we still franchise the self-ordained rational freedoms of the Greeks, the liberties of the Roman citizen, and the freeborn rights from the Levellers of the English Renaissance to Marx, Pisarev, and Malcolm X.

Most influential to 20th Century Judeo-Christian democracies and their interstate highways was Martin Luther King's vision of the franchise. King created a powerful democratic justice claim by aligning the mission of the State to Mosaic and Christian morality. An argument for consistency between the heavenly and earthly cities here emerged in deracinated equality to complete the obligation to God. As King's democratic Christianity led not to a mighty stream of human justice, we may doubt that justice is the truth that history bends toward. But this doubt is in fact power: we need neither discount the legal victories of the Movement nor rest upon them. We merely need to rescue their memory from numbing and restore a standpoint of horror from which democratic life may be renegotiated.

Lucan, a peculiar Silver Age Latin poet forced by Nero to commit suicide before he turned twenty-six, shows one mode of embodying a fraught virtue while doubting the arc of history. Writing in an era when the concept of Roman freedom had fallen into decadence (Lucan and Nero were both cultivated by Stoic education), Lucan showed that without heroes, the mythos of the state is destroyed. In Lucan's depiction of the civil war between Caesar, hero of Imperial order, and the Stoic paragons, heroes of Republican "liberty" (a war won by Caesar's army on the field of Pharsalus), both ideologies are undercut by the fountains of gore that parody the wills of the heroes. Scholars still debate whether the text's ambivalence is the result of Lucan's fear of punishment by Nero or a failure of skill. But the poem's power resides in its glimpse of sub-rational order. The enemy is not to be found among the actors. *De Bello Civili* finds its power not by favoring a moral order but in inventing a new kind of public reception of history as enslavement without end.

History, for Rome, was the story of power, the rationale for which is that individuals benefit from organization, administration, and command. The opposing ideology, usefully represented by the classical Stoicism of the Roman elite, held that self-control and individual virtuous action (*virtus*) were the only true ways to remediate the inevitable failure of power to avoid tyranny. Lucan's refusal of both of these inclinations leads not to abjection nor to classical Stoicism (its liberal apotheosis the appeal of Voltaire to cultivate your own garden), but to a performance of the vulnerability of citizens to ideology itself. Virtuous acts are profaned in a hollow, horrified vision in which all the historical meanings where *virtus* might reside have collapsed. The center of Lucan's tale of civil war is his engorged imagination of a thousand mutilations of the human body well beyond the mechanically possible. A bitter form of wit, the design serves not as decadent entertainment but as a catalyst to the end of the structures of history, with their false promises, their teleological hoaxes. Caesar's inhumanity is offset by an equal inhumanity beheld in the Stoic paragons. After he's lost the war, Cato follows his Stoic faith, refuses his soldiers the rights of surrender and return to their families. Cato's army flees through the mutated "Libyan sands," a nest of poisonous snake-creatures generated, eons ago, from the blood of the Medusa. In the soldiers' grotesque death march, snake-bit men ignite in flammable pus, drink their own blood, inflate and explode: the reward of Stoic virtue is spectacular punishment. *In se magna ruunt.* Greatness will outreach itself. Power erupts into tyranny, which begets new forms of protest and revolt to restore the basic human need to live rationally and justly with others within social orders and forms of power. It's ultimately true that the weight of any history will force it to fall, like a tree grown heaver than its roots will hold. But to turn that fact into abjection is to give way to decadence, however "stoic" this appears. The only hero that emerges in *De Bello Civili* is the enraged author straining to identify hope with the disgust of history, to return numbing to horror, as in that shock we generate temporarily the ontological standpoint of rationality itself, from which tyranny and freedom both reach.

I am trying to relate this thought to Tennessee, inching through an Arby's drive-through, talking into a digital recorder: In the twenty-first century the security state justifies its own terror in order to protect our right to not be afraid. We must cry freedom from the liberties the state seeks to secure. We must understand a precarious virtue unblinded to the more obscure truths of cosmos, that there is no end and no beginning but strife. Like Lucan, we cannot easily laud the victories of our most virtuous, as virtue, too, is absorbed in the illegible violence of the State. From Black Liberation's ideological ground of legislated equality we must now reimagine the revolutionary subject for the time we are in, why ignore this lodestone of revolt, visible under the ice sheets of commodity. The arc of the universe does not bend toward justice; instead, it shreds in the catastrophes of the state. We must find the voice that whispers fear in the same breath as love.

SEPS CARNIVALE

Look deep into my envenomed eye—
Cato doesn't care for the death
of Cato.
A corpse feels no pain.

All of you follow me
up the needle
to the source of the drip.
Prep the top of the hand
for intravenous pans
of hot machine oil

now up to the knees in
our ordinary occupations of the soldier
on Aff-
    ric march.

Any suspicion, don't
not pull the trigger.
Just set weapons around
corpses,

coat the kitchens and bedrooms
with non-violative incendiary
and run like hell—
If the obscurant don't burn them out
the offspring will drop by delayed birth defect.

Running like hell,

I lost my buddies.
White phosphorous
glows in aerial release

if I remember—

we farm the blood
of the Medusa's neck
as Perseus flew overhead—

one by one we
ignited in putrefaction

innovations in funereal practice
liquefying bones and body

from the poisoned carnival
of deadly snakes
mutated from Libyan sands.

From here, the story:
We few, fleeing the rule
of Caesar

occupied the town
in given testimony

responded only when
we took effective fire,
if I remember.

Jim, he got bit, only his gear
was left by the small fire
as the poison burned through his veins—

Deangelo, his eyes pancaked
when the venom pushed the sockets out.

We hurried from that boy's
tumescent corpse

and more and more bitter shrubs and cracked rock dust
    under us
by contract of private military consultancy,

on the hunt for vegetable lamb
with two armored support vehicles at

$600 a day.
I, it happens, the only human winner
on last year's *Man versus Beast* (Fox).

It was I who defeated the chimpanzee
at the obstacle course,
I who have seen a buddy beg
for the goods of his household
netting his intestines with his hands

as all my labor
drained away
as I hung from the light pole

that came on anyway
on a bridge crossing the Euphrates.

I die here unready
for war without war,
taking fire, on resource security detail

a soft target
such as pickup trucks and individuals
with no radio support

and nothing to contemplate but this clear plastic tubing's
    plip
        plip
           plip—

What fire looks like
in the veins.

I walked with Cato
barefoot among the snakes,

the *cerastes*, whose bite
ejects the spine from the body, and

the *iaculus*
that snake flies like an arrow.

Multifocal necrotizing presents.
O, *humanum modum*—
I quest the pure pus
welling from cavity of

the dying god
who dies when I die
in Libyan sands,

but I complain not.

We were taught to hate ourselves
in tight gymnasiums,
not cry out when the church windows
are shattered by bricks.

I will not cry out, but I am held back
by my body,

like the forty-four dwarves pulling an airplane.

I remember
only the elephant
knew honor the day of that shoot.

It's in the way of my eyes.
But no complaint have I against the desert womb:

birth is agony
and the way of open days would always lead
back to pain. Freedom from the way
is He inside me—

if I fear,
the fear in my open mouth,
it vomits Him.

What happens to me, to you, to all of our children
here with us this basement
is what Grace makes.

The *haemorrhois*, its bite
ejects the blood,

but the *dipsas*,
his venom,
it dries up—

I watch my skin turned to rime—

  at the water dyed with carrion blood
  a thirst so raking
I lay on my belly to drink with the snakes

then open my arm to drink
its sepsis.

FIELD BOOK:
BIRMINGHAM

In lower Alabama the ray-finned alligator gar grows to ten feet, survives on land for hours, and is favored by bow hunters because it brawls before dying. I note this in the Birmingham public library, driven in by a light rain from walking the infamous downtown streets where police dogs and fire hoses repressed protests. I share the library table with two African-American men in their sixties, retired, trading theories of the Nephilim of vast creative power, and off to the side, a lone white kid, about thirteen, taking studious notes on *Battleships of History*.

Earlier, when I entered Birmingham's Civil Rights Institute I was told by the retiree volunteer staff that I should hurry, the intro movie had already started. I pushed through a heavy curtain into a darkened space and stumbled into a gallery with a hundred hushed children sitting on the floor.

They had just been silenced by the image projected behind me—a double lynching of young black men at whom a mob of clean-dressed white men and women in skirts smiled and pointed. A girl at my feet gasped as I burst in, my head blocking the bottom of the video projection. I staggered to stop myself like Frankenstein's monster, sitting on the floor among the kids. On the screen, the excited faces of the whites seemed to think that lynching was better than a barn dance. The kids around me were too agitated to look away from me until the film continued into the 1950s, setting the stage for what the museum defined as the active phase of civil rights history. Finally, 1980s images of black middle class life raveled behind the credits, and the screen lifted to reveal the entry to the first exhibits behind, a little piece of stagecraft executed well enough to excite the kids into rushing forward. I remained seated as the lights came on, feeling exposed. I caught myself worrying that the kids would see only my race. I walked the galleries worrying over something else, something more trivial and perhaps more difficult to see: I was embarrassed by becoming a public body in a public testament to American slavery and its endless racial violence. I didn't know how to talk to anyone else in the galleries, the guards, the bookstore clerks. My body stared back at me in the restroom mirror, nothing to say.

API ETOILE (APPLE)

Wildness
    stalks the floor
we never run out of:

black granite squares
    flash frozen at sea, walking black windows
lit with rain;

    Bottom's up, night's cup
put on your mind *les*
        etoiles a-
            coil.

QUELLE

GER.: ''SOURCE''

It is convenient we can't find it.
I was a child found standing
 in the backyards of the neighbor
peering through vinyl windows
    of a garage.
The Dreamer naturally thinks that
    what she found
        is what she has lost.

HANGDOG

Tiger cells

overlap
down the hallway

talk goes by
cone by cone

productive
modes
seeing us home

Holly don't
go down

to the synod
of the cave

Holly don't
behave

in any way
I might recognize

"Holly"
"Holly"
behind you

I chew my
dew claw

CURBING

Ascenseur, Monsieur?

photons travel free   through angled cuts
in towers   the lush lawn
suddenly curbing   the edge downtown
where you are stopped   hear the little noise
one makes improvising   learning

LESS WHITE

I'm broke. I have a 4 year old and 23 month old that needs food in their bellies. Right now we have enough food to last up to the end of August. My soon to be ex hasn't helped with anything since he left. He took our supplies with him when he broke in to try to find stuff to sell. I was smart and hid our rifles and guns at my cousin's house. I'm afraid that tomorrow that I'm going to the local welfare office to apply for food stamps and maybe a check to tide us over until I find a job. Does this make less a WN if I get food stamps or a check? I just feel less white just thinking about it.

Unaltered post by Anonymous, June 18, 2009. stormfront.com, online forum. Note: "WN" is their parlance for "White Nationalist."

FIELD BOOK: SELMA

Morning overcast on State Highway 8, cutting through the mild green blur. Painted fences decry the United Nations, the US government, and taxation on rabbits sold for meat. It was a four-day walk from Selma to Montgomery. Imagine doing this while watching the fringe of the trees for a rush of field-deputized citizens to drive in with baseball bats. Road markers designate where the marchers camped to end the poll taxes and nonsensical tests (how many bubbles in a bar of soap?) that barred "Negroes" from the vote. The radio is a visible layer on the windshield. A station dedicated to the Southern Soul sound of western Mississippi and Alabama lost signal during a live recitation of cuts of the hog I can't picture. I pass three markers where the marchers camped roadside, and at each marker I have forgotten all of them, the kids, the young and elderly, still on foot back in 1965.

I stop to examine the soil at one of the markers near a farm. I think of blood, waste and hair of marchers that has been taken up as nutriment by the dirt, extirpated by plant energy, and laid into the soil again as waste from the marchers, the poor whites, and the Chickasaw and Choctaw peoples here in what Europeans called the Yazoo lands. The land changes without memory. The Cahaba lily is a long-legged spider amaryllis that grows in the swift Cahaba River from Birmingham down to Selma. The large bulb needs shallow, fast waters to lodge long enough in the shoals and shoot the big flower out in the river. Once adorning the river in flowers, the Cahaba lily is now endangered as river damming comes even to this sparsely populated part of the state. In the early 1960s, a black man trying to register to vote in the South risked being murdered with impunity, murdered by whites for even showing up on Election Day. Whatever I write on this landscape, I keep this written on my white face.

Parked at the lip of the Edmund Pettus Bridge, I drank a shiny blue liquid called "Relief Water" and tried to imagine the melee of that first attempt to march and the savage beating they found at the police cordon. King had equivocated on the march, sensing that white Selma was too easily provoked to an extreme violence that might backfire on the movement should the white public blame the activists for being too provocative. With King's absence, the New York media and photographers were sparse, and, in that absence, the assault more severe, with many of the marchers lucky to live. I think of King's label "inborn fear" to describe the almost unnamable destruction in the heart of the child taught to hate herself because she is black. This fear shadows the heart of race in America and is grafted to the hearts of the humiliated held in American torture sites across the globe.

A kid with a tricked out BMX bike cruised so slowly by he was barely upright, his underpants a pillowy ruffle above jeans belted below his butt. A man dressed in a plain t-shirt and sweat pants strode beside the traffic for eight minutes to clear the bridge before entering the convenience store. I noticed a marker for an unseen civil rights boardwalk below the bridge and followed the wooded, kudzu-bearded planks down toward the embankment of the Alabama River. My last act in Selma was to read awhile down in the heat, my eye caught by glints from a tipped beer can in a parked pickup under the bridge.

ROXBURY RUSSET
(APPLE)

Maple, ash, and service
raked up to my waist,

a silver sun
brings the place

to its senses,
Russets and

Leathercoat
in cold storage

the months now
I scope

branch
breaks,

amuse dolphins
found in the pen

book small wonders
of the basement

dancing before the half-open eye
on the wall of the whale

in cold ocean
looking to eat—

fine sharp particles
travel the ducts

a Roxbury shadow at mid-
day's reverse—

candid birds
under the minaret

in its gutter
a squat flame

waving Hi

BALDWIN (APPLE)

What in rice raises
pilasters of San Diego

a pen left in the belly
convulsing upward
years to break through the rightness or wrongness of
    traffic lights—

purchased by the Wheatley family

raised as Phyllis
in Massachusetts

poems praised by George Washington

never once talked about slavery
are slave poetry

IDENTIFY CRAFT

It's widgeon

dabbling tannin
pools in

this the leaf-enamored
marble
mine

LIMBS OF THE APPLE
TREE NEVER DIE

nec longum tempus, et engens
exiit ad caelum ramis felicibus arbos,
miratastque novas frondes et non sua poma

VIRGIL, BOOK II, GEORGICS

—Even Virgil heard
the limbs of the apple don't
know how to die;

you can freak a plane tree
to branch with fruits not its own,

but don't try breeding a Delicious
from seed,

the apple forgets its kind
to what chance did
and what it won't

—You'd spit nine soppy scions
from ten of any cultivar, or
rip the roof of your mouth with it,

yet any cow-browsed, rocky tilth
may yield a wild marvel's
Sheepnose, Baldwin, Ashmead

—To utilize the earth
choice apples must be found,
named, and securely lashed to the
forest drained of accident,

trees of tongue graft
whipped to root stock
coagulated with asphalt

for more fat, happy branches startling the skies
of Ecuador
in no time at all

—*Come and learn*
blessed is she

who prevents the unknown
desires of wild greens
by *Italian husbandrie,*

come and learn
it should hurt,
extracting host code
from graft

to acquire some synthesis
lashing bone
to cracked bone

in steroid pathways
at the lab

—The lore your fathers farmed
goes with you

as you go with who you are,

the genius of the soil
in howling competition

on the spiral arm of styrene pills
to Anchorage, Halifax, Shanghai

immunosuppressant skull helicopters

circling your cubicle
with the grace of complex coastal currents

never not a language to establish, enforce and
benefit themselves,

in heat-buckled parking lots
acting wrongly
as the matter
at hand

—A wave imitates wave
in the aquarium,

as you carry the aquarium
to the car,

a chore folded carefully from
branch to home

stitched with franchises I can barely see,
unable to move my head
under flaring spirals of ram's horns

drinking water and the fattening mud at
the mouth of the dawn,

faint, singed rose cups
touched back on lavender sheet,

on the morning drive

the yield of the mind
all principle orchard

organized by selective favor
of the regulation cascades

what you don't
and what you do
cut back

—Should the mason bees collapse
fell a brawny bull with rubber mallets

and leave the skin unbroken
to sun-boil

bowels to liquid,
the pierced hide spews

biosynthetic pathways of social force
flow as cells into new dumb root,

we follow in cosmic fantasy
the sky the one machine
turned on
to destroy itself

that is always
on

—No one taught the apple how to die
and none were taught the song
of self-assembly,

it sprang from the disemboweled shell
of a turtle the baby Hermes hollowed
and strung

and how the lopped tongue danced
from its beak
to the guitar of its body

—Little help
to the pyramid of boys lashed together

sodomized by the spotless feet of
stags in uniform
presenting the badge,

what it tortures out
and what it
won't

perfectly legal
expansions for husbandry

—Let the seed speak all it knows
in the ruin of its breed

as no better security exists
than for the dead

JOEL FELIX

LIMBS OF THE APPLE TREE NEVER DIE

Joel Felix *Limbs of the Apple Tree Never Die*
ISBN 978-0-9889885-0-7 $15
Order from Verge Books
1324 N. Wicker Park Ave.
Chicago, IL 60622
vergebooks.com

SPITZENBURG (APPLE)

The soil thumps like a belly
up the Hudson.

Follow the sound Sojourner;
avoid fracturing
fugitive joy—

A sorbate star and I
sow Esopus'

cart-wheel
arch-
itecting.

GEOMETRIC CLOSE

Map startled birds
as you find yourself wandering
the upholstered sphere.
The yew trees lend a curtain that
comes down to like minds.
Extirpate toxin from needles
and bark for your tea
for polyps bear arms in every gable,
five pennies a pound.

                    I can see now.
I can see.
It's not about having power:
Think of Titania taking
a long look at who is using her realm
to attempt mating
with long, solid, rock shapes.
That's her life.

                    With horror

I opened the tool box. Hope was
to raise manageable chunks
from the ice sheet
. . . but when at last they were spotted,
the penguins had given up.

So Titania goes home, something clicking
in her leg. Titania, parts of water
in a river slide with other parts
of a river
downward.
Go into the building
that doesn't finish as predicted
by the base.
Follow the arrows, then turn around.
The arrows follow you.

THE MIRROR HOLDS
MORE THAN THE ROOM

FOR CSR

Of tidiness and clarity, bites resolved
to the upright fraction
in remorse. A planet made of diamond
is discovered walking
the polar surface.
All directions reside
in continuous forced air,
venting in time, your body,
longer on its side, turned to the shoulder,
touching the light in the rim of the room
where the mirror begins.

A sound, meaning no harm
bounces when you move everyday rhetoric. The room
diffracts in dumb blades
of the fan. You and I,
through the blades,
bound to be,
a squeeze function stating it this way:
a staggering drunk
held between two cops walking into a cell
also ends up in the cell.
You watch me sleeping,
dragged in by you and my invention of you.
We pass the breath to each other
sleeping it off.

We are two distant dots, therefore
possible. The sun slipped off
its mask. I crawled forward,
a tiny red vein in the yolk of the egg.
I was both heads of a red and blue
snake joined at the anus,
long immune to my own bite,
a flying invertebrate bird. Speech
ran in the tracks
of the mind. The morning
broke powder. I drank.
A skin that cannot be wetted
walled the flower.

What King Saul saw in the mirror: God's
withdrawal.
The torment of the body that followed.
No meds or court songs
dulled the edge,
but for the voice of a rude shepherd
and his bony guitar.
How the moist breath of the boy
caressed his king.
David, your song
opens this room, binds the twins
of the mirror's reverse.

Rolling calabash runs the tracks of
human migration. Two
cups of milk, seized in the esophagus,
have been planting the self,
all along.
The principal remedy is to worship
the blood in the vessel
of reversal. Help us
out of our water, follow the meres
back to the sea.

SAWYER (APPLE)

Old sun, the world is thy
   curtain

Come on down
   to meet me
       tonight

FIELD BOOK:
MONTGOMERY
BUS STATION

I lingered in Montgomery, walking the empty downtown on a humid Saturday morning. I entered King's Dexter Avenue Church but couldn't bring myself to go down to the pews. In Rome, I was never uneasy about exploring the naves of every church; here, it felt like a blasphemy to Christianity's role in civil rights. I was waiting for the National Civil Rights Memorial to open its doors, slowly winding up to the state capitol building, and finding a monument to the Confederate dead crowning the hill. I looked down to the city. The morning haze sat down on the city a bit more. As I drifted back to the car, I noticed a small crowd gathering. I found it was a public announcement of plans for a new monument for the Freedom Rides that ended here at the now defunct Montgomery Greyhound station. I couldn't believe my luck; the vivid courage of those brave enough to use the 1960 law banning segregation on interstate travel to challenge state segregation laws never released my imagination. The terror of those trips, stalled by burned out busses, TNT attacks, slashed tires, clan beatings with pipes, bicycle chains, baseball bats, and finally, the police-protected beatings on this very ground, lives, submerged, in your body. In 1961, the Freedom Riders rode in an empty Greyhound en route to Montgomery. Any random passengers had long since given up their tickets to avoid being attacked along with the Freedom Riders by the mob waiting in Montgomery. Given that the mob had hospitalized many in Birmingham, and had tried to storm the hospital to beat the wounded during the night, the Freedom Riders legitimately believed they would be killed by the mob when they pulled into Montgomery. By chance, no one died. The white mob attacked the photographers and reporters to eliminate witnesses before turning to the beating of the Freedom Riders. Today, a few of the original Freedom Riders were assembling on the street as the heat turned up another notch and the older, well-dressed ladies fanned themselves. How young they were even today, some only in their fifties now. I joined the crowd jealously eyeing the thin shelves of shade provided by the facing store lines.

Microphones were tested and replaced. The row of Freedom Riders waited patiently in the thickening heat. I suddenly realized not one was older than my own father. Seeing through black and white film archives created a sense of ancientness to the Movement that has to be undone, I realized. I was tapped on the shoulder. A white woman roughly my age asked if my name was Joel Felix. "What?" I blinked at her. "Hey, we met years ago in graduate school," she said. Nervous but focused students buzzed around her with digital cameras and lighting gear. "Wow, right, so do you live in Alabama now?" I asked, stalling in the hope of recalling details. "I'm teaching at Syracuse. I'm doing a class on activist art and brought my class here to film the Return of the Freedom Riders to Montgomery . . . Wait weren't you in Chicago?" "Yeah," I said, "I came down from there to think about the civil rights movement." "Awesome," she said. One of her students had a pressing camera issue and tapped her foot once in anxiety. The Freedom Riders were being cued to tighten up the line in front of the bus station for photos. I stepped back from the students, and it began only then to dawn on me, as I was told repeatedly in the opening statements, that this was the actual site of the building and parking lot where the Freedom Riders were stopped. The standing structure's outline was the old

Montgomery Greyhound station, now to be restored and revitalized as a visitor center, linked with the Rosa Park's home and museum just a few blocks away. I was standing in front of the parking lot that saw the brutal public beatings that nearly took so many lives. I found a place to crouch in the shade where I could stare in wonder at the Freedom Riders seated to the left of the podium as lawyers, grant writers, and representatives spoke, driven by an embarrassing hunger to connect to the courage that lay beyond the representation of their experience we were watching. After many minutes it began to seem that no speeches were to be given by the riders themselves, and though I felt no disappointment, I was soon walking away. The street had been blocked off for the public event, and, as I left, a pickup came by, windows down, and seeing the barricade and the nearby podium and crowd, the white driver, unshaven, about my age, looked me in the eye and said hotly to me, "They've got to be fucking kidding." He whipped the wheel and threw his arm back to reverse, the engine slipping the transmission with the violent shift. In a jerky, squeaking three-point, he gunned off.

DULCET (APPLE)

queued
    rosaceae
russeting
    malus
shelter-in-place
    blackbird
thrush
    Apollo's big
apples
    an open habit
beneath trees
    entheo-
gen
    soil flows
of whose
    eucharist

THE PLEAS OF PANDA

Panda space is everywhere
vulnerable, empty
of color and full
of atypical matter.

Strange; the fact is,
we once were comfortable
in these facts,

rings of darkness
that cannot be seen

without remorse,
late nights
on the bed of dead bees.

*

In my life
also began

me, the subject to
evidence.

I visit him at work
cutting the inevitable bonds
in the day's
tetchy tissue.

Not much stands in the way:
A trail around trees
peeling from the wall
dispensing soda
and panda screaming.

*

All music in this folder
is a curious thesis
on illness.

Food is placed in my mouth
Expense it.
It is expensive,

the stupor dance.

*

Others may be called
before you
from an area
not visible within 2C.

This, too, can be destroyed
when it grows up,
when the nest is brought down.

                    *

Now touch
individual pieces of attached
stuff, the necessary gaps
for operation of each
oiled syllable,
the fear
that holds the sky.

AQUI VIVE

Glass clouds
birch brace

sparrow shot

into a new world
I bring familiar poverty

THE GOLDEN LOOM

1

Brown and
blue
rivulet stepped through
vows of coots
down from the mouth—

tears are running on the water
as Friday Creek
   rids itself of its
place
-ment

2

It has been this day already
all over the world

way West—
the bent light
is rinsed thin

waxwings musing

How do they do
that aluminum moon?

3

Held
in Friday Creek's

weather
-seized
   extensive

4

And how do they do
living skin
set out back

on this portable
screen

with Friday Creek left
—ajar

FIELD BOOK:
PORTLAND

It will seem as if these words come from nothing, but they do not. A March snow deliquesces to sticky rice on the bed of the leaf. The snow breaks down, *contritus,* its walls ground to water, and air carries the vapor away. In the leaf ladle all that remains is the great vibration, the dragging metal and milk of this place, noisy eructations of its flesh and fruit, the indenture of morning. Between the twigs, invisible airwaves crackle with life; the air talks as radio to storefronts poked from the evergreens, oil refinery a vacuum tube on the circuit of earth. It is a diapason—at once —the anaplastic mammatus askance. The channels are hailed to irreducible facts sliding within a fictive set of dimensions, a toy universe for how heavy were the gods when footprints of Zeus crushed small cars to the sea bed; irreducible, like a shore, like what's fucking freezing, like plates of the mountain snapped outward. And in that volume lies the demon of freedom. Freedom, our bantam god, swiftly kicks up the fantasy to be in my own bed again at last, gaining leg lock on my lover, our limbs unhinged with lack of obligation. Freedom is the condition of Portland converted to hunger, the apologia of identification, a pattern become familiar that someone once saw and cut out of the mind on this window, the vertical cloisonné roads are drawn to, the rife crown of the regnum walking the lighted edges of a leasehold whose vulnerabilities outlive its ruin. It is the stars on their leashes in the waiting room, the page crossed by a breath, branches' shadows on bare walls. In freedom we issued from Mother's back, the words by thousands, weightlessly swimming images of appearance, events made of the silence filling the oven, the pinecone spanning the throat, the plast of autopsied omens pulled from the box that walks the six feet of body walking down the hallway, open to a street blasting from its kernel, rooms populating furniture no one touches or sees on the reaching skin of the word, shambling there, crying?

SPARTAN (APPLE)

Alder falls
and parched grass
on the pass
flying trash
and *spiritu*
sipping Sprite

blinking
red light

underfunded hills
the sword fern
sporulating
in plain air

*

I like big orange
birthday cake
at dawn

there are robins
it's the vernacular

hearsay
for siskin and clover
and the jack pine
making creative use
of difficult plots

white-bellied swallow
on blue wing
little quizzing
how thicket fits
get a bit
runic

*

Building slivers
driving by
self-playing chip

fine wood fiber
aloft
spun by the trees

this shoreline is
all it needs

*

Plastic mechanicals pump
a rough line of grass
topped by ivy shine

custom plantings then
hedge apple

a dying ant
calls for a Jubilee—
for cancellation of debts

flocking the sky
with no hope and no desire
of escaping
temporary-ness

VOLCANO INFO

Insert thought
in fold / proceed
with slot

what do the words
want

organized cascades
going wide

colors emitting
light

in rebar, EVAC
guides

bumping blue
pile,

lexical throbbing
patch
reception-red

roots
inquire locally

geography is Nature

time
depreciates

what doesn't fit
on a blue tarp
must be forgotten

lava flowed over this table
for three million years

on the lake-followed
road

FIELD BOOK: CHICAGO

Migratory juncos, sapsuckers, yellowthroats, buntings, and ovenbirds found stunned, one leg stirring the air, bird head torn from body otherwise intact, birds with one wing at first light on the sidewalks downtown and popped in the trash not long into morning. Birdspotting at dawn from corpses crashed into the glass towers at night. Summer's truck dust and cottonwood rattle the bed of air incalculably vertical, as if the city could fall off the side of the green ball, as if that height called the skyscrapers to stand by the lake. The yellow tassels of the honey locust tips shaking above the grey road. The long black husk of the pod finally dried by October, crunching underfoot, the loosened beans freed to mark what will be swept away, with these faces, this desiring army of quick-turning finches. The caged pigeon with a broken neck somehow alive, feeding and cooing from its upside down head, nursed by my Mexican neighbor in dense Pilsen under the roaring el. The rapid paper shutter of its black bean eye, the sky, opening and closing under me.

WINTER BANANA

(APPLE)

When summer slows up
blush flushes under the wax

as thin, hard fingers of the tree
oblate the points
of pyri, bake tight
rocks of heat to
test the soil's nectar
there where your thigh turns inside.

Pieces of human emotion
short watercore
until the master dies.

Until the master dies
please don't stop releasing

information from me
in fine black seeds

plant-derived wrappers
thick, idiot, fruit
carried here
the whole fleet
fucking in the hold.

I AM WRITING

I am writing from the Bubbly Creek
I have a crush on you, my
Lord, who pushes up wild carrots
from this bed. I pop them out
for the sighs of the mud,
the gassy music of decay
from your glass nipple muttering.

POUND SWEET
(APPLE)

When the rain breaks

flex wall topples
the pool into the room

an instance of good keeping
hissing surf stones by the pound
once
brought in pippin

The first threads of this book came from exploring conditioned origination in the apple tree. Each wild born apple, as Virgil understood it, "forgets its former juices" and the color, form, mouthfeel, and flavor of the fruit that takes place can be seen as a kind of performance from the probabilistic field at the site of germination. This frustrates human consumption, and conquering the wildness of the pome by grafting branches of choice fruit to unproductive trees was a virtue of Roman culture to be spread through didactic poetry. In the apple poems I was practicing some kind of ancient field poetics by grafting constituencies of democratic violences and fleeting fantasies of liberty in the languages of everyday performances, uncontained but conditioned by geography.

Once the poems took up the concept of origination, it was obvious that the site of origination was only partially external; it was also the place of enframing. I stumbled into another dimension of modern field poetics, which had proposed that the poem is a dynamic field of psycho-physical-historical interaction. As I do not conclude that I live outside of the ambivalent violences of everyday life, I could not forget that poems are inside the making and unmaking of those violences. The Field Book entries broke into the manuscript to pose further interpenetration between the fantasies of subjectivities in our social formations and the production of the poems. This seemed to be a way to revive the tool of referentiality as a dynamic field of influence on critical consciousness. The waning of "representation" within radical poetry's recent history has calcified once-dynamic engagement with the social relationship of poetics and, in the terms of rhetoric, abandoned the role of common suffering in ethos and identification to the conditions within which we all emerge, feeling with tender antennae for the ability to respond. Should I accept that any form of poetry fails as revolutionary action (as I do), I cannot relinquish the claim that the art should remain responsive and responsible to the common suffering of culture. And if every politically motivated representation is a fiction, we might not lose sight of how all fantasy is formed under the pressures of systems dictated by democratic violence.

The efficacy of poetry to catalyze revolutionary subjectivity can neither be proven nor disproven. Is it not enough to remain open to inchoate imperatives, to honor the urge for a place where passion meets in common consciousness? Perhaps the means of identification from within the paradoxes of critical art is through a double framing of the life of the art within the life of violence, disclosure of the dependent co-production of human capacities arriving from rational transparency, despair and faith. If this were possible, the poem might remain awhile in the inchoate, lively in the potential to identify itself with a revolutionary subject as yet unknown.

In the time of this book I lived in Chicago, moved to the Pacific Northwest, and traveled as I could within the violence of "freedom" as understood in our time. This is the best of my responsibility to writing some parts in that field of view.

ACKNOWLEDGMENTS

Some poems appeared in other form in *The Cultural Society*, *From a Compos't*, *Fifth Wednesday*, and *LVNG*. The author of the remark on Cairo, IL is GOP Missouri state representative Steve Tilley. On Lucan, see W. R. Johnson's study *Momentary Monsters: Lucan and His Heroes* and Frederick Ahl's *Lucan: An Introduction*. Some lines in the book in reference to apple grafting and wild apples were gathered from Virgil, Liberty Hyde Bailey (1858–1954) and Thoreau. I owe a special debt to Kristina Chew's visionary translation of *Georgics*. "Seps Carnivale" references some of the outlandish serpents in Lucan's poem, definitions of legal combat in the US Army *Manual of Warfare*, and the bizarre public record of an American soldier of fortune killed and dismembered in Fallujah in March 2004. I'd also like to note that the Field Book reports started in correspondence to Candice Rai and Wallace Whitney, and that an early appearance of some of this text was printed as a catalog accompanying an exhibition of Whitney's paintings.

None of these poems or their antecedents would have been possible without the love and support of Chicago:

Swimming in my hat
and what
I thought
out in the lake I did enjoy
the buoy's break and
the bright company
lighted there

JOEL FELIX

was born and raised in the Downriver Detroit area.
As an adult, he settled in Chicago where he co-edited
LVNG magazine for ten years. He holds an MFA
from Bard College and presently serves as an
Associate Director of Curriculum in the University
of Washington's School of Public Health. He lives in
Seattle with Candice Rai and their son Sanchaman.
This is his first book-length collection.